FAITH OUT LOUD SAMPLER TWO

Discipleship Ministry Team
Ministry Council
Cumberland Presbyterian Church

November 2015

**8207 Traditional Place
Cordova (Memphis), Tennessee 38016**

©2015 Discipleship Ministry Team

All Rights Reserved. No part of this book may be reproduced or transmitted in any form or by any means, electronic or mechanical, including photocopying, recording, or by any information storage or retrieval system, without permission in writing from the publisher with the single exception that purchase of this curriculum grants the purchaser the right to copy and distribute student handouts within each lesson for use in their local church. For information address Discipleship Ministry Team, Cumberland Presbyterian Center, 8207 Traditional Place, Cordova (Memphis), Tennessee, 38016-7414.

The Discipleship Ministry Team of the Ministry Council of the Cumberland Presbyterian Church is the successor organization to the Board of Christian Education of the Cumberland Presbyterian Church.

Funded, in part, by your contributions to Our United Outreach.

First Edition 2015

Published by The Discipleship Ministry Team, CPC
Memphis, Tennessee

ISBN-13: 978-0692567876
ISBN-10: 0692567879

We want to hear from you.
Please send your comments about this curriculum to
the Discipleship Ministry Team at faithoutloud@cumberland.org

OUR UNITED OUTREACH
Made Possible In Part By Your Tithe To Our United Outreach

FAITH OUT LOUD

CORRIE TEN BOOM
BY WHITNEY BROWN and ANDY McCLUNG

SCRIPTURE
JAMES 2:14-26, GENESIS 22:1-14, JOSHUA 2:1-24

THEME
When they're born from true compassion, our prayers for others lead to action.

LEADER INSIGHT

CONNECTING TO YOUR STUDENTS
Any honest assessment of American Christianity must conclude that we've had it pretty easy. It's probably hard for your students to grasp the idea of being physically beaten for possessing a Bible, or risking one's life to attend worship.

This lesson will showcase a completely foreign world.

Even if your students have studied the Holocaust in school or learned of it from a book or movie, its horror and terror is still difficult to grasp. A quick web search for holocaust images would be disturbingly enlightening. Like Mr. Rogers said, though: when seeing images of scary things, look for the people helping. Corrie ten Boom and her family were those helpers in the midst of perhaps the most atrocious act in history.

Your students may engage in intercessory prayers regularly. They may do regular mission work. But do they recognize the connection between the two actions?

EXPLAINING THE TOPIC
Corrie ten Boom was born in Holland in 1892, the fourth child in a Christian family. The family ran a watch shop out of their home, but had little money. From her parents, Corrie learned that prayer and hospitality are parts of being a Christian, and that the Jewish people are special to God. She accepted Christ at the age of five, and thereafter was known for her compassion and intercessory prayers, both of which usually focused on people the world saw as unimportant—the drunks stumbling home from bars on her street, those with mental developmental issues, her poor or Jewish neighbors. Corrie was also an early proponent for women, beginning girls' clubs for teens to have a place for recreation and spiritual growth.

In the 1930s after the Nazi party took over their own government in Germany, they began to invade neighboring countries. In 1940 they took over Holland. Corrie was in her 40s and running the family watch shop. German soldiers soon were everywhere. Then food was rationed and curfews imposed. Then the persecution of the Jewish residents began. "Jews Forbidden" signs went up; Jewish-owned shops were closed; and all Jews were forced to wear the star of David. Then the Nazis started gathering up Jewish people and sending them away from their homes. No one knew, at first, that they were being sent to concentration camps to be murdered. No one could imagine that six million Jews would be murdered before the war was over.

Corrie's family took in Jewish friends, neighbors, and strangers to hide them from the Nazis. This turned into an organized local underground resistance movement, hiding dozens of refugees in various homes and sneaking them out of the country when possible. Corrie and her underground workers also helped German soldiers who deserted after realizing Hitler was evil.

Corrie worked out a complex system with the underground. A certain sign in the shop window would mean it was safe to enter, and information was exchanged in coded conversations right in front of Germans. Eventually, Corrie began coordinating with the broader underground resistance movement. They were the ones who sent men to smuggle in tools and materials to build a secret room in Corrie's house. When Nazi search parties came in the shop, someone would sound a hidden buzzer. The refugees would quickly enter the hiding place through a sliding panel under the bottom shelf of a bookshelf. Seven people often hid in this room, which was only thirty inches deep.

In February of 1944, it all fell apart. The Nazis knew Corrie was harboring Jews. They knew about the underground network. The shop and house were raided, but the hiding place wasn't found. Corrie and her sister, both in their 50s, were beaten, arrested, and sent to prison. Their father, 92, was arrested too. He died ten days later. Other family members were arrested and released. Guards were stationed at the house, but the people in the hiding place escaped.

Imprisoned in her own country, Corrie still treated others with kindness, other inmates and guards alike. One lieutenant, after Corrie talked to him about Jesus, destroyed files taken from Corrie's house that would have gotten many more people arrested and executed. This same man tried, unsuccessfully, to get Corrie and her sister released.

As the Allies advanced into Holland, Corrie and her sister were moved to concentration camps in Germany. Corrie managed to smuggle in a Bible. She used it to bring herself and others encouragement and comfort in that horrible place. She often broke camp rules, risking beatings or death, to help others.

Late in 1944, Corrie's sister told her that after the war God wanted them to open a healing center for concentration camp survivors. She died the next day from illness. Then, inexplicably, Corrie was released. Someone made a clerical error. Corrie took a difficult journey home, finding Holland war-ravaged but partially liberated. Knowing she was being watched, she couldn't work with the underground anymore. They raised some money for her, though. She reopened the watch shop and opened the doors of her home to the mentally handicapped.

> Corrie only learned of the clerical error in 1959 on a return to the camp to honor the 96,000 women killed at this camp. She was supposed to be gassed the week after her release.

When the war was over, Corrie started the healing center. Her criterion for knowing when someone was healed was that they could forgive. She also toured the country, speaking about the horrors of the concentration camps and the mercy of Jesus. Her popularity as a speaker took her throughout Europe and the U.S. People would often approach her or write her to say that during the war she had spoken words of encouragement to them, prayed with them, helped their loved ones, or that they had simply observed her compassion and faith, and had been moved to accept Jesus for themselves.

Corrie died in 1983, but only after her books about her experiences had become best sellers and a popular movie had been made from one of them. So even after her death, her encouragement to forgive and experience true compassion continues.

THEOLOGICAL UNDERPINNINGS
Pity is feeling sorry for someone in a bad situation. We can feel and express pity while remaining "above" the bad situation. Compassion is caring so much about someone in need that we can't help but to show them kindness. Compassion leads us to enter into the other person's misery with them. Corrie ten Boom practiced compassion, not pity.

Corrie also practiced an effective style of evangelism. She was bold and direct, but she didn't scream from a street corner, telling passersby they're going to hell unless they repent right now. Her actions of compassion and helping paved the way for people to hear her tell them the good news of salvation through Jesus. Her story is full of people whom she led to Christ who then led others to Christ. The secret of her evangelistic success may be that she did what she needed to in order to tell others about Jesus, but she didn't try to do the Holy Spirit's job. It is the Holy Spirit who convicts people of their sins and the need for repentance (see Confession of Faith 4.01-4.02). Also, she never seems to have tried to convert Jews into Christians, but respected that they are God's chosen people.

People in horrible situations—and it doesn't get any worse than living in a Nazi concentration camp—are more likely to turn to God than continue to rely on themselves or whatever they have been drawing on for spiritual support. Perhaps that is why so many middle-class American Christians' evangelistic efforts have been fruitless: they've been trying to evangelize people who are quite comfortable. Their efforts may produce more Christians (but not necessarily financially contributing church members) if aimed at the sick, the imprisoned, the addicted, the desperate. (Ironically, that Christianity lends itself to, and focuses on, the marginalized is one of the reasons some people criticize the faith.)

APPLYING THE LESSON TO YOUR OWN LIFE
Recall any stories from family members who witnessed the effects of the Holocaust, or any stories you know of it from your own reading and education. If you're unfamiliar with the Holocaust, spend a few minutes browsing ushmm.org, the website of the United States Holocaust Museum. Imagine what you would have done, had you been a Christian in a country the Nazis took over.

Have you ever been in danger of, or suffered, arrest or physical harm for doing what you believed was morally right? If not, for what beliefs would you take such risks? If so, were your actions born from a socio-political stance, or from a theological belief? Is there a difference?

Which do you pray more often: for God to "be with" people in need (sick, hungry, bereaved, homeless) or for God to use you to help people in need? Can we Christians be answers to our own prayers?

JUST IN CASE
If your students don't seem to recognize how they might help in a situation like the Holocaust, share this story: Before she was arrested, Corrie heard about a Nazi plan to raid a Jewish orphanage and kill all the babies. She told the teenagers of the underground to come up with a plan to save them. She didn't want to know details so, if captured, she couldn't give away the plan. The teenage boys, dressed in German uniforms taken from deserters whom the underground helped, pretended to conduct the raid and took the babies. The teenage girls helped every single baby find a new home. About one hundred babies were saved that day.

CORRIE TEN BOOM
BY WHITNEY BROWN AND ANDY McCLUNG

SCRIPTURE
JAMES 2:14-26, GENESIS 22:1-14, JOSHUA 2:1-24

LEADER PREP

RESOURCES
- Masking tape
- Video player for virtual tour
- Handout of bookmarks
- Copy of your church's prayer list
- Virtual tour of the Corrie ten Boom Museum (http://tenboom.com/en/)
- A small space (A square barely large enough for your group, taped on the floor would work. This is symbolic of the ten Boom's hiding place. See "Call to Wake Up.")

BEFORE THE LESSON
Review the link to the Unites States Holocaust Memorial Museum to prepare yourself for potential questions your students might ask about the Holocaust.

Tape an appropriately sized square/rectangle on the floor to create your "hiding place."

Review the virtual tour of the Corrie ten Boom Museum, especially sections 8-13, and have it prepared to play on your media player.

Make as many copies of the bookmarks in this lesson as needed for your students on thick paper, and cut them before your students arrive.

Find a copy of your church's prayer list, and make sure you know the needs of the people listed.

GET STARTED

CALL TO WAKE UP
Create a small space, barely large enough for all of your students to fit uncomfortably, and conduct the majority of the lesson from within this space. Use items in your classroom to outline the space, or just use tape to make an appropriately sized rectangle on the floor.

As students enter the room, quietly rush them into the space.

CALL TO WORSHIP
Have someone read this quote from Corrie ten Boom on prayer:

"We never know how God will answer our prayers, but we can expect that He will get us involved in His plan for the answers. If we are true intercessors, we must be ready to take part in God's work on behalf of the people for whom we pray."

LISTEN UP (20-25 minutes)

James 2:14-26

14What good is it, my brothers and sisters, if you say you have faith but do not have works? Can faith save you? 15If a brother or sister is naked and lacks daily food, 16and one of you says to them, "Go in peace; keep warm and eat your fill," and yet you do not supply their bodily needs, what is the good of that? 17So faith by itself, if it has no works, is dead.

18But someone will say, "You have faith and I have works." Show me your faith without works, and I by my works will show you my faith. 19You believe that God is one; you do well. Even the demons believe—and shudder. 20Do you want to be shown, you senseless person, that faith without works is barren? 21Was not our ancestor Abraham justified by works when he offered his son Isaac on the altar? 22You see that faith was active along with his works, and faith was brought to completion by the works. 23Thus the scripture was fulfilled that says, "Abraham believed God, and it was reckoned to him as righteousness," and he was called the friend of God. 24You see that a person is justified by works and not by faith alone.

25Likewise, was not Rahab the prostitute also justified by works when she welcomed the messengers and sent them out by another road? 26For just as the body without the spirit is dead, so faith without works is also dead.

Activity: After reading the passage, divide your class into three groups. Assign each group one of the following readings, and ask them to come up with a summary together. The first two are the stories mentioned in the scripture above.

Group 1: Abraham – Genesis 22:1-14
Group 2: Rahab – Joshua 2:1-24
Group 3: Corrie ten Boom – allow this group to read from the "Explaining the Topic" section of this lesson plan to learn about Corrie's life.

After all three groups have finished reading and summarizing; ask them to share with the whole group.

DISCUSSION QUESTIONS
What stands out to you most in this passage from James?

How does Corrie ten Boom's life help you better understand James 2:14-26?

Can you think of a time when someone has showed you their faith by the way they treated you or someone else? What was that like?

DISCUSSION QUESTIONS

NOW WHAT? (10-15 minutes)

Activity 1: The Corrie ten Boom Museum has a virtual tour of the ten Boom house on their website (http://tenboom.com/en/). Take the tour with your students. The "hiding place" explanation begins on point number 8 in the tour. If you are limited on time, begin here and go through point 13. Point 13 is the actual "hiding place"; use the navigational arrows at the bottom of the screen to look at the full view of the small space.

Activity 2: Come out of your "hiding place." Invite students to share what that experience was like for them. How would their thoughts and attitudes about being in that small space have been different if their life and safety depended on staying there for hours?

While teaching this lesson, students may have questions about the Holocaust. The United States Holocaust Memorial Museum has resources available for teachers, including commonly asked questions: http://www.ushmm.org/educators/teaching-about-the-holocaust/common-questions

LIVE IT (5-10 minutes)

Look at your church's prayer list. Choose someone for whom you will intercede, either as individuals or as a group. How will you become involved in God's answer to that prayer?

Give each student a bookmark. Invite them to write the name of the person for whom they will pray and what they intend to do as a part of that prayer on the back of the bookmark. Tell them to take it with them to be reminded to be in prayer for that person.

Resources used in compiling background material: Corrie: the Lives She's Touched by Joan Winmill Brown, The Hiding Place by Corrie ten Boom, tenboom.org. Photos used: "Corrie-ten-Boom2" used from "A Christian Worldview of Fiction" - http://goo.gl/hKAanm, "Holocaust Memorial" by Milan Boers - https://goo.gl/qEmgnz, "Holocaust Memorial" by Milan Boers - https://goo.gl/8mVDb5, "Secret rooms in the library" by Marcin Wichary with coloration edits - https://goo.gl/7LYzo5

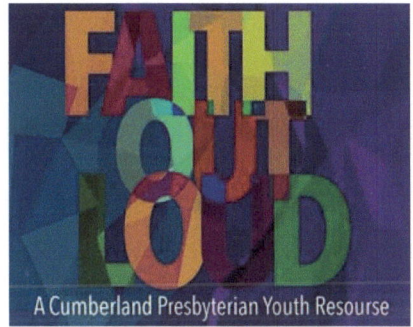

That's Not in the Bible?!?
by Andy McClung

Scripture: Varied

Theme: Some things we think are found in the Bible aren't actually there.

Resource List

- Bibles
- Copies of the handout "That's Not In the Bible"? one per student
- Pens, one per student
- Copies of "Is This in the Bible"? Pop Quiz, two per student
- Envelopes, one per student
- Pads of paper, one for every 2-3 students
- Enough space for break-out groups to work

Leader Prep

- Put one copy of the "Is This in the Bible"? Pop Quiz in each envelope and seal them.

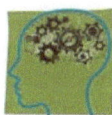

Leader Insight

Connecting to Your Students
Teens seem to enjoy being critical of everything—"critical" here meaning "inclined to find fault with something, often too readily." Nowadays, though, many teens don't seem to have much inclination, capability, or opportunity to be critical of anything—"critical" here meaning "skillful judgment/assessment as to something's truth, merit, or value."

For example, let's say a new movie opens tonight. That movie was likely announced more than a year ago. Teaser trailers and full previews have been shown constantly for the last eight months. Plot details, set photographs, and allegedly pirated video clips have been posted and reposted online thousands of times, and viewed millions of times. Bloggers and fans have already given the movie their thumbs up or down, before even seeing it.

Notes:

A couple of months ago, the studio gave a special early screening to professional critics, and they've published their reviews. So when teens sit down in that movie theater tonight, they've already been primed to like or dislike the movie.

Essentially, they've been cheated of the opportunity to experience and critique the movie for themselves. Constantly being cheated of this opportunity, they've never even learned how to critique movies.

This lesson, hopefully, provides an opportunity for teens to be critical (the finding fault kind) of certain misconceptions about what's in the Bible, while also encouraging them to be critical (the skillful assessment kind) of what's behind those misconceptions.

Explaining the Bible
Presented here is the same information from the "That's Not In the Bible?" handout, with additional notes to help you lead the discussion during the "Listen Up" portion of this lesson. This section, then, is longer than usual. Don't worry; you don't have to cover all of this information.

This lesson will cover three categories of things people mistakenly think are in the Bible: 1) physical things and/or their descriptions, 2) events and their details, and 3) sayings.

- Physical Things

Many people think that particular Bible-related physical items actually existed and therefore must be mentioned in the Bible, when they really aren't mentioned anywhere in scripture. Some of these physical things or beings are indeed mentioned in the Bible, but the generally held descriptions of them are not. These misconceptions and false images come more from art and poetry than from scripture.

The serpent in the Garden of Eden wasn't Satan. Genesis never states this. The idea of Satan as a tempter wouldn't even come along until 500 years after Genesis was composed. This idea probably came from our knowing Satan is evil, and our wanting to blame our sins on a tempter instead of acknowledging our weakness. (Genesis 3:1-15)

The forbidden fruit of Eden wasn't an apple. It could have been, but Genesis never states this; it's only called "fruit." This idea probably came from paintings of the scene as artists imagined it. A bright, red apple draws attention. (Genesis 3:1-6)

Angels aren't female, don't have wings and halos, and don't play the harp. The study of angels is too complicated to fully cover here, but all the mentions of angels in scripture refer to beings who look like men. They're bright, but don't have halos. The angels mentioned in the gospels are not said to have wings. The seraphim have six wings. See Isaiah 6. The typical image of an angel comes from painters. John Milton's Paradise Lost gave us the idea of angels playing the harp. Cherubs, the fat baby angels, are anything but cute. This image probably started when Renaissance sculptors adorned children's graves with images of dancing babies. Ezekiel describes cherubs (or cherubim) in Ezekiel 10:20-22. They have wings.

We don't each have a guardian angel. The Bible shows them bringing messages from God (Luke 1:26-38), fighting fallen angels (Daniel 10:10-14), and helping people (Daniel 6:22). The idea of personal guardian angels probably comes from Matthew 18:10.

People do not become angels after dying. There is nothing like this anywhere in scripture or in 6,000 years of Judeo-Christian teaching. Angels are immortal spiritual beings created by God separately from humankind. This idea was presented in a 1946 children's book, The Littlest Angel and in the 1946 movie "It's A Wonderful Life," but it probably predates both of those. The idea possibly comes from confusion about departed loved ones "watching over us" from heaven; the human inability to let go of departed loved ones; or a comforting idea of what happens to people when we die.

Satan isn't red, doesn't have horns, doesn't carry a pitchfork, and doesn't live in hell. There is no physical description in the Bible, but something that looked like this would have a hard time tempting most people to anything! All these ideas accumulated from images made by various medieval artists trying to visually depict evil. In Matthew 25:41, a character in a parable says hell was prepared for the devil, but not that he lives there.

The Holy Grail doesn't exist. Sure, Jesus used a cup at the last supper (Matthew 26:27) —the Passover meal uses five cups—but there wasn't anything extraordinary about it. The Grail and its magic powers were simply plot devices for the originally French story of King Arthur. The tale has been added to and changed countless times.

Notes:

Notes:

- Events

Many people mistakenly think specific details of certain events are mentioned in the Bible. This may be because so many artistic depictions include those details.

Scripture tells us a large fish swallowed Jonah. It doesn't say a whale, though it may have been one. Whales, of course, are mammals rather than fish, but those who first repeated and eventually wrote down Jonah's story may not have bothered to make that distinction. A whale may be mistakenly attributed to the story simply for its size. (Jonah 1:17)

Baby Jesus being born in a stable may or may not be accurate. The Bible only says he was put into a manger, which leads us to the (admittedly safe) assumption that the birth happened in a stable (Luke 2:6-12). Stables in that place and time were likely to be caves with a gate rather than freestanding structures. Also, the innkeeper who turned away Mary and Joseph is not mentioned in scripture, despite being portrayed thousands of times in Christmas pageants, sometimes as a greedy man who turns them away because they have no money, and sometimes as a compassionate man who allows them use of his stable. Either way, it's supposition.

There might have been more than three wise men, there might have been fewer; the Bible never gives a number. The idea of three probably comes from the three gifts they brought, but has been reinforced by tradition and a hymn, even to the point of giving them names, ascribing them ethnicities, and deciding who gave which gift. (Matthew 2:1-12)

Jesus didn't wear underwear on the cross. The Roman practice was to strip the victim naked, adding to his humiliation. Besides, scripture clearly says the soldiers divided up his clothes. The loincloth, not a Jewish undergarment, was probably added by artists for modesty's sake. (Matthew 26:35, Mark 16:24)

Saul/Paul may or may not have been on a horse when he was struck blind. Artists like to show him dramatically having just fallen off a horse, but scripture only says he fell to the ground. (Acts 9:1-9)

- Sayings

Many people mistakenly think certain Bible-sounding and churchy-sounding sayings are in the Bible. This may be because churchy, Bible-quoting people often use and repeat such sayings.

It may also be that we like bite-sized, easily-remembered, profound sayings. Some of these misquotes are simply paraphrases of real scripture. Some of these paraphrases are used to mean approximately the same thing as they do in the Bible, and some are not.

"A fool and his money are soon parted." Usually true, but not in the Bible. The phrase entered English after 1557, as a condensed form of a rhyming couplet from a poem called "Five Hundred Points of Good Husbandry," by Thomas Tusser, which read, "A foole and his monie be soone at debate / which after with sorrow repents him too late."

"Ask Jesus into your heart." This phrase, popular in some areas, isn't wrong, but it doesn't accurately reflect scripture or Cumberland Presbyterian theology. It probably comes from Revelation 3:20, and the subsequent paintings and hymns. Read it and you'll see that it's a big jump from that verse to salvation. Salvation does indeed come through Jesus. John 3:16, Acts 16:31, and plenty of other passages testify to that, but the key word is "believe." Salvation comes from God's grace. Our part is repentance, belief in Christ as Savior, and following Christ as Lord or master. Our Confession of Faith affirms this in 3.10. "Asking Jesus into your heart" is an oversimplified way of saying all this.

"Cleanliness is next to Godliness." Not in the Bible. It's possibly paraphrased from the Talmud (an ancient collection of Rabbinic teachings), and/or a sermon by John Wesley (1703-1791). Many passages in the Old Testament do emphasize physical, ritual cleanliness before approaching God. New Testament emphasizes spiritual cleanliness. See 2 Corinthians 7:1. This saying is sometimes misused to keep those responsible for cleaning house humbled or subservient.

"God helps those who help themselves." Not in the Bible. Attributed to Poor Richard's Almanac, 1736, by Benjamin Franklin. This saying isn't about God. It says we should take care of things ourselves because God isn't going to help. This is not only non-Biblical, but anti-Biblical. Leviticus 19:9-10, Matthew 25:31-46, and many other passages encourage us to help people in need rather than tell them to help themselves. This saying, however, discourages helping others, as if self-reliance can fix any problem and is our only hope. Much of the New Testament reiterates the futility in trying to live life on our own, apart from God.

Notes:

Notes:

It's also attributed to an Aesop fable in which a man with a stuck wagon prays to Hercules for help. Hercules appears and tells the man to get out and push, because "The gods help those who help themselves."

"God works in mysterious ways." Not in the Bible. It's a paraphrase of the opening line from the poem "Light Shining out of the Darkness," by William Cowper (1731-1800): "God moves in a mysterious way / His wonders to perform." The Bible does, however, repeatedly affirm that God's ways are mysterious—unknowable—to us. Ephesians 1:7-10, 3:3-5, Colossians 1:27. That's why the psalmist prays as he does in Psalm 25:4.

"Love the sinner, hate the sin." Not in the Bible. It's a paraphrase of a comment by St. Augustine in A.D. 424: "With love for mankind and hatred of sins." Also from Gandhi's 1929 autobiography: "hate the sin and not the sinner." The intent behind the saying is Biblically sound. See Romans 12:9 and Mark 12:31. This saying is a point of contention between conservative and liberal Christians. Each group seems to say the other group overemphasizes one half of the saying while underemphasizing the other half.

"Money is the root of all evil." Not in the Bible. It's a misquote of 1 Timothy 6:10, which says the "the love of money is a root of all kinds of evil" (NRSV). Big difference!

"Pride goes before a fall." Not in the Bible. It's a paraphrase of Proverbs 16:18: "Pride goes before destruction, and a haughty spirit before a fall" (NRSV).

"Spare the rod, spoil the child." Not in the Bible. This is a paraphrase of Proverbs 13:24: "Those who spare the rod hate their children, but those who love them are diligent to discipline them" (NRSV). The "rod" is the same as in Psalm 23, used to guide rather than spank. This proverb encourages teaching, guiding, and directing children, not spanking them as many take it.

"This, too, shall pass." Not in the Bible. It's possibly a paraphrase of 2 Corinthians 4:17, but just as likely a non-religious way of saying "hang in there."

Theological Underpinnings

A recent survey in the United Kingdom found rampant ignorance of the Bible in youth and children. Less than a third knew what Good Friday commemorates (although that's not necessarily in the Bible). Only one-fourth knew what Easter celebrates. Judas being Jesus' betrayer was known by 75%, but only 33% knew about that kiss. More than a third of children thought "The Tortoise and the Hare" was in the Bible. Why so much ignorance? Well, this same study revealed that 71% of parents with kids 3-16 said their children had never read, seen, or heard the Easter story. If they're not teaching their kids that story from the Bible, it's a safe bet they're not teaching them anything from the Bible.

But that's overseas. American kids are much more Bible-literate, right? Well, during Lent of 2014, a North Carolina church staged a passion play. They built and used an outdoor set of a tomb, complete with costumed Roman soldiers standing guard. According to the pastor, passers-by kept asking if they were reenacting a scene from the movie *Gladiator*.

Biblical ignorance is even a problem within the Church. We hear something that sounds old and wise, and assume it's Biblical especially if the saying reinforces what we already believe, such as "God moves in mysterious ways." Sadly, many people who claim a love for the Bible don't read it. Their exposure to scripture is limited to Sunday school and worship or quick devotionals with very little scripture. Thus, bits of folk wisdom and old sayings end up taking on Biblical authority in their lives. This puts the person in control of (presumed) scripture instead of allowing scripture—or, more precisely, the Holy Spirit working through scripture—to be their "authoritative guide for Christian living" (CP Confession of Faith 1.05).

Applying the Lesson to Your Own Life

Which guides your life and decisions more: old sayings or Holy Scripture? If you answered "scripture," are you sure your favorite, guiding passages really are from the scriptures? Which are you more likely to quote in public, scripture or an old saying?

What are some old sayings that you find timelessly true? What are some you find ridiculously outdated (not the language, but the message)? For these latter ones, were they ever true, or were they wishful thinking?

Recall a time when you realized that one of your long-held beliefs about something being in the Bible was wrong.

Notes:

Notes:

How did you respond? Did the way you approach scripture change?

Consider making a list of Bible-sounding, but not Biblical, sayings that you often hear, and then search scripture to find an actual verse that says the same thing. Next time someone uses the non-Biblical saying around you, you can respond with, "Or as the Bible says…" and see where the conversation goes.

The Lesson

Get Started (10 min.)

As soon as all students have arrived, announce that you're giving a pop quiz. Ham it up by saying the church session wants to know how well you're doing as a teacher (which, technically, should be true), or that you're thinking about starting to give grades for this class, like in school (you just thought about it, so this isn't a lie either).

Hand out pens and copies of "Is This in the Bible?" Pop Quiz, but have them keep the quiz face down.

Announce that students have 90 seconds to complete the quiz. Have students turn over their sheets, write their name on it, and begin. Every 15 seconds, call out the time remaining. When 90 seconds is up, call out "Pens down!" and collect the quizzes. Without revealing the correct answers—all the answers are "no"—grade the quizzes in front of the class and announce each student's grades. When all grades have been announced, reveal the correct answers and the fact that you've been kidding about the grades.

Ask: **Are you surprised? Which of these did you really think had to be in the Bible? Which of these did you know right away wasn't in the Bible? If these things aren't in the Bible, where do they come from?**

Explain that in this lesson the class will explore some of the things people mistakenly think are in the Bible. But first hand out the sealed envelopes with the "Is This in the Bible?" Pop Quiz copies inside. Explain that there is a copy of the quiz in each envelope and that the students are to find someone an elder, parent, grandparent, pastor, teacher —to give the quiz to in the coming week. Remind them to have a pen handy and keep the quiz sealed until someone is ready to take it. Students are to report back at the next meeting what happened.

Listen Up (20 min.)

Distribute the "That's Not In the Bible?" handouts. Work through the lists however you wish. You could go straight down the list, or pre-select which ones to discuss. You could ask students which items draw their interest, or which they're most familiar with.

Use the background information above, under "Explaining the Bible," and the discussion questions below to help you lead the discussion of each item chosen. Have a student look up and read aloud the indicated scripture, if there is one, for each item discussed.

Possible discussion questions for each item covered:

- Why do you think people think this is in the Bible, and why has it stuck?

- Have you ever heard anybody say that this is in the Bible? In real life? In a movie/TV show?

    Did you believe them? Why or why not?

- Who is most likely to believe these things are in the Bible: church-going, Bible-reading people, or people who don't read the Bible?

- What can we as a class do to teach people that this isn't from the Bible?

Notes:

Notes:

Now What? (15 min.)

Divide the class into small groups of two or three students each.

Give each group a pad of paper, a pen, and a Bible. Explain that each group is to come up with a new saying that sounds like it comes from the Bible. They can completely make up something, paraphrase a real Bible verse or Biblical concept, combine two Bible verses or concepts, or anything else they want.

The saying should be short and easy to remember. But let's avoid making any more of those Biblical-sounding sayings that actually contradict what the Bible says. These should be phrases that actually support Biblical principles.

Give about ten minutes for groups to work, and then gather the whole class back together. Have each group share its new saying.

Groups should only give explanations about their sayings if asked because the sayings should be understandable at first hearing.

Have the whole class vote on the best of these sayings, allowing some slight editing if necessary.

Lead the whole class in repeating the new saying several times, until it is memorized.

Encourage students to use this new saying as a verbal bonus question when they give the pop quiz to someone this week. Students can reveal the source of this new saying after revealing the correct answers to their test-takers.

Live It (5 min.)

Close the lesson by saying: **A lot of things people mistakenly think are in the Bible are good advice, or uplifting, or helpful in some way. That's why people think they're from the Bible. God is the source of all good things, and all good things point to God. The Bible does too. But let's always do our best to know what's really coming from the Bible and what's just coming from people.**

Resources used: archive.org, cnn.com, dictionary.com, thetimesnews.com, What the Good Book Didn't Say by J. Stephen Lang

© 2015 Discipleship Ministry Team of the Ministry Council of the Cumberland Presbyterian Church. All Rights Reserved.

Notes:

Digging Deeper:

For almost 400 years, most English-speaking Christians read and used the same version of the Bible—the King James Version. In certain circles, anyone misquoting a Bible verse or misattributing an old saying to the Bible could count on being corrected quickly. The last 50 years or so, however, has seen dozens of new translations and paraphrases. While this new scholarship is good and makes scripture available to those who struggle with outdated language, it has also caused some confusion. Now, when someone misquotes scripture or mistakenly attributes an old saying to the Bible, they are less likely to be corrected. Others who suspect a mistake may keep quiet, thinking the speaker is quoting from an unfamiliar translation. It will be interesting to see if even more non-Biblical but Bible sounding sayings emerge because of this and are passed on.

"Is This in the Bible?" Pop Quiz

1. Adam and Eve ate an apple from the one tree God said not to eat from.
   ☐ Yes   ☐ No

2. Satan and his demons live and rule in hell.
   ☐ Yes   ☐ No

3. "God works in mysterious ways."
   ☐ Yes   ☐ No

4. Baby Jesus was born in a stable and used a manger for a crib.
   ☐ Yes   ☐ No

5. "This, too, shall pass."
   ☐ Yes   ☐ No

Key
1. No
2. No
3. Yes
4. No
5. No

"THAT'S NOT IN THE BIBLE?!?"

These physical things and descriptions are NOT in the Bible
The serpent in the Garden of Eden was Satan. Genesis 3:1-15.
The forbidden fruit of Eden was an apple. Genesis 3:1-6.
Angels are pretty females, with wings and halos, playing the harp. Seraphim and cherubim do have wings, but aren't pretty. Isaiah 6, Ezekiel 10:20-22.
We each have a guardian angel. This idea might come from Matthew 18:10.
People become angels after dying. There is nothing like this anywhere in scripture.
Satan is red, with horns, carries a pitchfork, and lives in hell. See Matthew 25:41.
The Holy Grail. See Matthew 26:27. The Grail was a plot device for the story of King Arthur.

These events, or details of events are NOT in the Bible
A whale swallowed Jonah. See Jonah 1:17.
Baby Jesus born in a stable, and the innkeeper. Mangers are most often found in stables, but the Bible never mentions a stable. The innkeeper is never mentioned. Luke 2:6-12.
There were three wise men. Matthew 2:1-12.
Jesus in his underwear on the cross. He would have been naked. Matthew 26:35, Mark 16:24.
Saul/Paul falling off his horse when struck blind. No horse is mentioned. Acts 9:1-9.

These sayings are NOT in the Bible
"A fool and his money are soon parted."
Adapted from a poem by Thomas Tusser, 1557.
"Ask Jesus into your heart."
Salvation does come through Jesus, though. See John 3:16, Acts 16:31.
"Cleanliness is next to Godliness."
Adapted from ancient, non-Biblical Jewish writings and/or a John Wesley sermon.
"God helps those who help themselves."
Actually contradicts Leviticus 19:9-10, Matthew 25:31-46, and many other passages! Attributed to Benjamin Franklin (1736) and/or an ancient Aesop fable.
"God works in mysterious ways."
Paraphrase from a 1700s poem. The Bible does, however, repeatedly affirm that God's ways are mysterious (unknowable) to us. Ephesians 1:7-10, 3:3-5, Colossians 1:27. That's why the psalmist prays as he does in Psalm 25:4.
"Love the sinner, hate the sin."
Paraphrase of a comment by St. Augustine (A.D. 424) and Gandhi (1929). Agrees with Romans 12:9 and Mark 12:31, but not in the Bible as we say it today.
"Money is the root of all evil."
A misquote of 1 Timothy 6:10. Big difference!
"Pride goes before a fall."
A paraphrase of Proverbs 16:18.
"Spare the rod, spoil the child."
Paraphrase of Proverbs 13:24. Misused to condone spanking children.
"This, too, shall pass."
Possibly a paraphrase of 2 Corinthians 4:17, but just as likely a non-religious way of saying "hang in there."

LEADER INSIGHT

CONNECTING TO YOUR STUDENTS
Your movie-loving students may be aware that Wonder Woman is supposed to appear in some upcoming movies. Your comic book readers may know her. Although she's consistently been around since 1941, your other students may only have heard of her.

Your students may think there is nothing, outside of math and (maybe) science, that's unequivocally true. This may shock you, or you may be right there with them; it depends on your age. The last few generations have grown up in a world that gives equal value to all opinions, and harshly criticizes anyone who doesn't. An opinion doesn't even have to be an informed opinion to have value. "Is that true?" is considered archaic. Now it's, "Is that true for me? Is that true in this situation?"

Truth is important. Salvation through Christ is not an opinion, provable scientific fact, or a solvable math problem. But it is truth—an eternally important truth.

EXPLAINING THE TOPIC
Wonder Woman wasn't the first female superhero, but she was the first to achieve popularity and longevity. She first appeared in All-Star Comics #8 in 1941. At the time, women in comic books were rarely anything more than love interests or damsels in distress for the male heroes to woo or save. Wonder Woman broke this mold. She is extremely strong, resistant to damage, can fly (originally in an invisible jet but later on her own), and a skilled warrior. She wears bracelets with which she can deflect bullets in flight. Plus, she carries a magic and unbreakable golden lasso.

In the days when most superheroes were created by young men, Wonder Woman was created by William Moulton Marston, a middle-aged psychologist and women's rights activist, at the request of a publisher who wanted to quiet the criticism that comic books were too violent. Marston pitched Wonder Woman as a character based on love, beauty, and truth rather than masculine violence. He believed a strong female character would both attract female readers and show them that they could do anything. Those early years of Wonder Woman, though, sent mixed messages. Sure Wonder Woman was strong, capable, and independent, but she also ran around in a skimpy costume and was frequently tied up by men. The skimpy clothes might have been to keep male readers interested, but Marston said the bondage scenes were only to show Wonder Woman later escaping—literally from the ropes or chains, and metaphorically from the bonds of male-imposed gender roles. People are still debating if Marston was more feminist or fetishist.

Her origin story says Wonder Woman doesn't fit the mold of the stereotypical 1940s American woman because she was raised in an all-female society in which all roles— leaders, warriors, nurturers—are filled by women. She comes to our civilization to return a male soldier who crash-landed on this secret island home and to share their superior values with us. She is introduced with: "At last, in a world torn by the hatreds and wars of men, appears a woman to whom the problems and feats of men are mere child's play." Early stories show Wonder Woman, disguised as Diana Prince, confused by our world with all its war, hatred, crime, and tension between genders.

Some superheroines are just copies of male characters (She-Hulk, Batgirl, Supergirl), but Wonder Woman is mostly original. Marston did draw from Greek myths about a race of fierce warrior women called Amazons. Female supervillains were already around (Batman's foes Catwoman and Poison Ivy), but when Wonder Woman's archenemy Cheetah was introduced in 1943, readers saw two super-powered women fighting for the first time.

Wonder Woman's lasso is particularly interesting. When around someone, it forces them to tell the truth. Marston would go on to invent what eventually became the polygraph, or lie detector. (Marston's device only measured blood pressure. Polygraphs measure multiple physiological reactions.)

Truth is powerful. Step 1 in twelve-step programs is to recognize the truth: "We admitted we were powerless over alcohol—that our lives had become unmanageable." Until an addict, anorexic, bulimic, or abuser recognizes and admits the truth, there can be no healing. This is why confession has long been a part of Christianity. As long as we maintain the lie that we're not sinful, we can't be forgiven (1 John 1:8-9). A comic story in 2000 revealed that Wonder Woman regularly uses her lasso to reveal any lies she's telling herself so she can stop. She knows she can't fully be who she's supposed to be with self-deception in her life.

Lies, or untruthfulness, breed more lies. Unfaithful spouses, upon being caught, often express relief because managing a web of lies is so stressful. Telling the truth is much easier.

Nowadays many people consider truth to be subjective. What's true for you might not be true for me; what's true in one situation might not be true in another. Thus, nothing is absolutely true. Stepping onto a lake, however, ends up with somebody getting wet, no matter how strongly they believe they can walk on water. Someone with the opinion that the grumpy lion at the zoo just needs a hug will need a lot of stitches and several units of blood. In a 2002 story, Wonder Woman's Lasso of Truth is broken in battle, resulting in all truth dissolving. Whatever people believe becomes truth: the moon is made of cheese, 2 + 1 = 4. This story affirms the ridiculousness of thinking our opinions or beliefs shape truth. Instead of thinking that, we're better served to allow truth to shape our opinions and beliefs.

Mike Brewer highlights the saddest aspect of subjective truth: "If the only truth is my own beliefs, then I will never find a truth bigger than myself." He also says, "Truth can set us free, but opinions cannot."

THEOLOGICAL UNDERPINNINGS
Some people confuse truth with fact. Facts are indeed true, but truth is bigger, more spiritual, than mere facts. If you brag about taking second place in a foot race but don't mention there were only two runners, you've spoken fact, but not truth. The statement "God is good" is true, but can't be proven as factual. That it's the opinion of millions of people isn't what makes it true.

God created men and women "equal and complementary" (Confession of Faith 1.11), designing each gender to need the other. As much as some try to say there's no difference between men and women,

the truth is there are some things each gender is generally better at doing. People who deny this, blame culture for limiting gender expectations into children, but even atheists recognize specific gender roles in humankind. For example: men became hunters because, on average, they can throw a spear harder and farther than women and wouldn't have to leave the hunt to deliver or nurse babies.

We cannot save ourselves. As much as we'd like that to be false, it's true. Cumberland Presbyterianism was partially born by breaking away from strict Calvinism, which says we have no say in our salvation. CPs didn't go so far as say it's completely up to us whether or not to accept salvation, though. We believe God calls us to salvation and gives us the faith to respond to that call, but it's still our own free will choice.

Before Pilate, Jesus said he was born and came into this world to testify to the truth, adding, "Everyone who belongs to the truth listens to my voice." When Pilate asked, "What is truth?" Jesus didn't respond. He'd already told his disciples, "I am the way, and the truth, and the life". (John 18:33-38, 14:6)

APPLYING THE LESSON TO YOUR OWN LIFE

Plenty of movies and live-action TV shows have featured male superheroes. To date, Wonder Woman has appeared in only one live-action TV series (1975-1979), and no movies. There have, however, been several failed TV pilots and movie attempts. Why do you think it's been so hard for Hollywood to bring Wonder Woman to the screen?

Do you think men and women could do everything equally well if, from childhood, both genders were equally taught domestic and nurturing skills, how to emote, and physical assertiveness, or are there inborn differences between the two genders that significantly affect behavior?

If Wonder Woman lassoed you, what question would you most fear she might ask?
Do you believe some things are true, regardless of what anybody thinks about them or what can be proven? If so, what are some of those things? If not, then how do you define truth, and what did Jesus mean by calling himself "the truth"?

DIGGING DEEPER

Lots of research shows that, on average, men and women are far more alike than different in personality, psychology, cognitive ability, and sexuality. Where they differ in these areas, they differ by small margins. Those small margins, however, sure seem to cause a lot of conflict. Differences in grip strength and running speed are only slightly greater. Where men and women differ significantly, on average, is muscle mass and strength. Perhaps because this difference is so universal, there are fewer conflicts over it.

WONDER WOMAN AND THE TRUTH
BY JIMMY BYRD AND ANDY McCLUNG
SCRIPTURE
JOHN 8:32, JOHN 14:16, JOHN 18: 33-38, 1 JOHN 1:8-9

LEADER PREP

RESOURCES
- 2 pieces of paper for each student
- Pencils or pens
- A hula hoop
- Newsprint or dry erase board and markers.

GET STARTED

GET STARTED (10 minutes)
Have each student write down on a piece of paper two things about themselves that are true and one thing that is false. After everyone is finished, pick one person to read their three statements. The rest of the group must figure out which one is a false statement. Give everyone a chance to read their three statements.

Ask: How easy or hard was it to deceive each other with your one false statement?

LISTEN UP

LISTEN UP (20 minutes)
Say: Today we are learning about truth. Chances are, since you were a little kid, you have been told to always tell the truth.

What if there was a magical device that when it touched you, it made you tell the truth no matter what?

Say: Wonder Woman is a superhero from DC Comics and also a member of the Justice League. She has many special powers including: super strength, ability to fly, incredible combat skills, and resistance to harm.

> There is a complete background on Wonder Woman at the beginning of this lesson by Andy McClung. You may want to share in more detail about Wonder Woman to those who are not as familiar with her.

Say: One really cool thing that Wonder Woman has is a golden lasso that when wrapped around someone, makes them tell the truth.

Place a hula hoop on the floor. (A yellow or golden hula hoop would be perfect!)
Ask for a volunteer to stand in the hula hoop. Explain that when standing in the hula hoop, they will be asked 5 questions, and they have to tell the truth.

First set of questions for volunteer
1) Have you ever fallen asleep in church?
2) Have you ever cheated on a test at school?
3) Have you ever disobeyed your parents?
4) Have you ever peed in a public pool?
5) Are you a One Direction fan?

Second set of questions for another volunteer
1) Have you ever thrown up on a fair ride?
2) Have you ever had a crush on Justin Bieber?
3) Do you believe in ghosts?
4) Have you ever sneaked out of your house?
5) Have you ever stolen anything?

Ask: Was it hard to tell the truth? These were fairly easy questions to answer truthfully, but what if it had been very personal questions to answer, and the hula hoop really was a magical device that made you tell the truth?

Ask: Why is telling the truth so important?

Say: Now here is a deep question: What is truth?
(Your class may have various answers on what they think truth is; make sure and listen to each one.)

DISCUSSION QUESTIONS

Say: Let's look at what the Bible says about what truth is, and then we will answer the question again: What is truth?

Have someone read John 8:32, another person read John 14:6, and another read John 18:33-38.

Say: After hearing these three passages read, can you tell me what truth is?

Write down answers on newsprint or a dry erase board. Give the class time to discuss their answers.

NOW WHAT

NOW WHAT? (10 minutes)
On the supernatural TV show "The X-Files," their slogan is "The Truth is Out There," which corresponds to the two main characters who are always looking for the truth in the midst of conspiracies and paranormal events.

OPTION 1: Give each student a piece of paper and something to write with. With the previous scriptures in mind, have them each write their own slogan about truth. After everyone has finished, have them share their slogan with the rest of the class.

OPTION 2: Have students draw or paint a slogan about truth. Let them be as creative as they want to be. When they are finished, have them show the rest of the class.

LIVE IT

LIVE IT (5 minutes)
Read 1 John 1:8-9 to the class. "If we say that we have no sin, we deceive ourselves, and the truth is not in us. If we confess our sins, he who is faithful and just will forgive us our sins and cleanse us from all unrighteousness."

Say: We are obviously not perfect, and we will make mistakes and not always tell the truth. Does that mean that God loves us less? (No!)

Close with prayer, giving your students time to pray silently and confess any lies they may have told; Close with this declaration of pardon:

"The mercy of the Lord is from everlasting to everlasting.
I declare to you, in the name of Jesus Christ, you are forgiven.
May the God of mercy, who forgives you all your sins,
Strengthen you in all goodness, and by the power of the Holy Spirit keep you in eternal life." Amen.

(The Service for the Lord's Day – Supplemental Liturgical Resource 1 - Pg. 53 – 1984 Westminster Press)

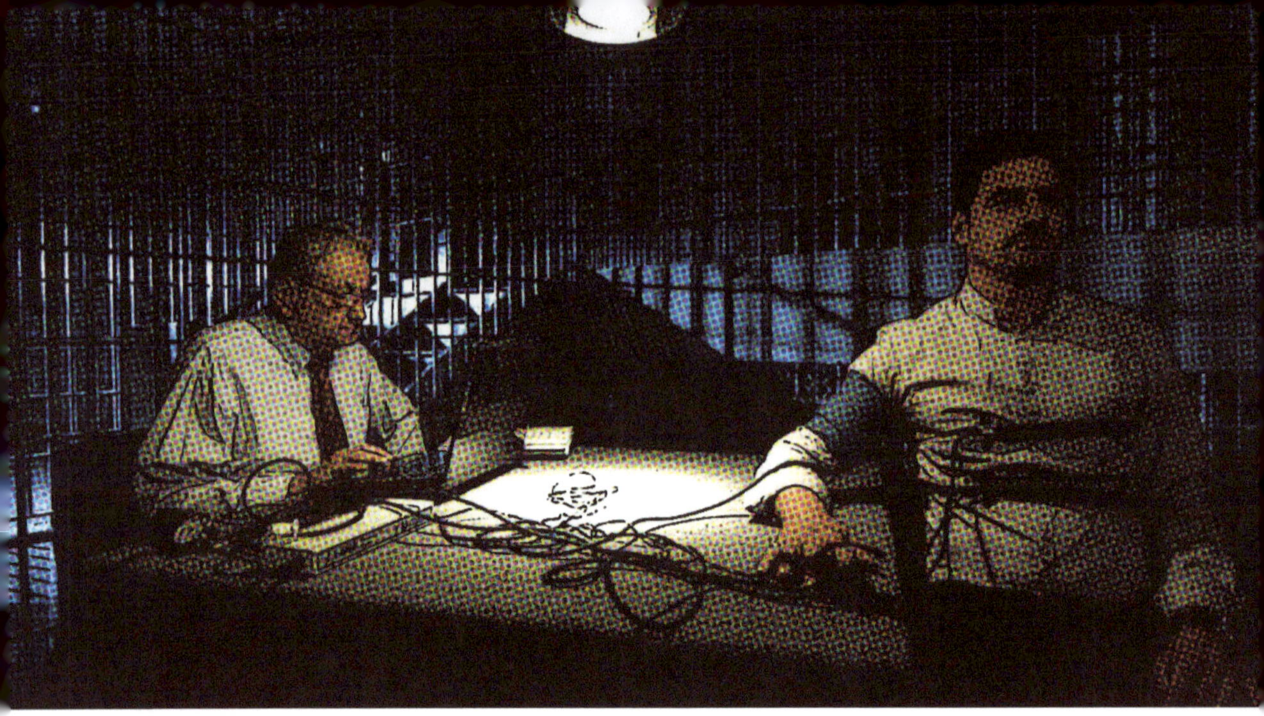

NOTES

Resources used in compiling background information: Alcoholics Anonymous 4th ed., Comic Book Character by David Zimmerman, comics.org, dccomics.com, dictionary.com, imdb.com, npr.org, The Psychology of Superheroes edited by Robin Rosenberg, "Understanding the Mysteries of Human Behavior" by Mark Leary, Who Needs a Superhero? by Michael Brewer. Pictures used: "1978 Superman & Friends Greeting Cards" by Mark Anderson with edits of comicbook actions - https://goo.gl/g12LDb, "Speak the truth, even if your voice shakes" –Maggie Kuhn Cringle Park, Levenshulme, Manchester" by Duncan Hull with edits and comicbook actions - https://goo.gl/PmLkYN, "Lie & Truth Sign" by geralt with edits of comicbook actions - https://goo.gl/Mk9hz2, "Lwp Kommunikáció" by Próbára tett profik (Alexis Conran) with edits of comicbook actions - https://goo.gl/JVFvSI

Colossians:
Back to Your Roots
by Whitney Brown

Scripture: Colossians

Theme: In Paul's letter to the Colossians, he speaks with urgency, reminding the church of who Jesus is and what that means for the lives of those who follow him.

Resource List

- Video: "Knowing My Identity" from Bluefish TV
- Video capability (laptop, projector, DVD player, speakers, etc.)
- Song: "Beloved" by Derek Webb
- Music player (laptop, MP3 player, CD player, speakers, etc.)
- Lyrics to "Beloved" by Derek Webb
- Newsprint
- Markers
- (Optional) Paper and markers, crayons, pencils for "Listen Up: Option 2"
- Strips of cloth (bandanas work well)
- Permanent markers
- Hairdryer
- A brick (or rock or box of similar size and weight)

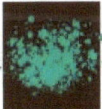

Leader Prep

- Find the song, "Beloved" by Derek Webb.
- Load the video, "Knowing My Identity," available on YouTube from Bluefish TV. (http://www.youtube.com/watch?v=iBGaGxppGkl)
- Display the lyrics to, "Beloved" by Derek Webb. Write questions on newsprint as listed in the "Get Started: Call to Worship" activity.
- Gather paper and writing utensils for "Listen Up: Option 2."
- Cut bandana or other cloth into strips about once inch thick and 6-12 inches long.
- On the brick (or rock/box), write the list of qualities found in Colossians 3:12-17: Compassion, kindness, humility, meekness, patience, forgiveness, love, peace of Christ, thankfulness, wisdom.

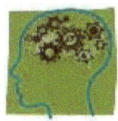

Leader Insight

Connecting to Your Students
Students today are surrounded by identity thieves. Overwhelmed by the competing ideas of such a variety of religious beliefs, both within and outside of Christianity, on top of the

Notes:

appealing calls of media and consumer culture, it is easy for students to be caught in the wind without even realizing they are being carried away from the heart of the Good News. Paul speaks to a similar situation in his letter to the Colossians. The letter is a great overview for students who are trying to grasp the full scope of the Gospel. Paul outlines it clearly for the Colossians so they are not swayed by other teachings that may sound good at first, but fall short of these gospel truths. Students today are surrounded by just as many, if not more, competing philosophies. This study of Colossians will help them better understand their roots and why it is important to remain firmly planted in them.

Explaining the Bible
Paul is writing to a community of Jesus followers whose identity is being threatened by the spread of false teachings and philosophies. Due to this threat, Paul writes with urgency and with great purpose to strongly summarize and remind them of the Good News— the core Gospel truths of who Jesus was, what he did, why they follow him, and how that discipleship should change their lives. Paul leaves the Colossians with a concrete understanding of the way they must continue living as people reconciled to God.

Colossians 1:
Colossians begins as a Pauline letter with an opening, a greeting, and thanksgiving for the community to whom he is writing. This particular letter was written while Paul was in prison, likely around the same time as his letter to the Ephesians. In Chapter 1, Paul begins to outline his reason for writing, reminding them of their spiritual roots, the sovereignty of Christ, and how it has completely transformed their identity. Christ followers have been transformed from strangers and evildoers into a reconciled part of Christ's own body, "holy and blameless" (v. 22). Therefore, they should live accordingly.

Colossians 2:
Chapter 2 continues in reminding the Colossians of their former state and the complete difference receiving Christ has made in their lives. Readers also find out the issue that prompted Paul's letter in this chapter: false teachers and their regulations that should have no reign over believers.

Colossians 3:
Paul does not spend a lot of time complaining about these false teachers and going into detail about what they have been teaching and how it is wrong. Instead, he goes into de-

tail about what the life of one "raised with Christ" will and will not include. He begins with a list of habits that should be put to death and never revived. If we feel we have this list under control, we will no doubt find something we can improve in his second list. Verses 12-17 describe a wardrobe of holiness— traits our lives should radiate as followers of Christ.

The end of Chapter 3 and beginning of Chapter 4 gives instructions for wives and husbands, children and fathers, slaves and masters. These verses will raise questions for your students as they have for centuries in the church. It is important to understand Colossians 3:18-4:1 within its setting. The Word of God must never be used to oppress any person or group of people. The point of Paul's letter to the Colossians is freedom, finding their identity in Christ, and helping them understand reconciliation. There is no room for oppression. So, what is with these verses?

Remember that Paul is writing a letter. A letter is for a specific person or group of people in a particular time and place. The Colossians are part of a patriarchal culture. Men lead families and society, and some households have servants and slaves. Paul writes to the Colossians in this context, not because it is the ideal context or because it should forever remain the same, but because it is their current reality. Paul gives them instructions on how to live within this lopsided society. If we consider the three groupings- wives/husbands, children/fathers, slaves/masters, we see a common denominator. Although Paul has instructions here for wives, children, and slaves, he is not really telling them anything new or outside of the norm for their society. Paul outlines for the wives, children, and slaves what they are already doing, and explains they should do these things well and so serve God. Essentially, "Do your best to serve those you have the opportunity to serve. Do it as service for God." However, the husbands, fathers, and masters are called beyond their cultural role. They must also respond with service, love, and fairness to those in their care. This is their duty, not from the society that would place them at the top to do as they please, but from Jesus, who calls all to serve and love God first, and then one another.

Colossians 4:
The rest of Chapter 4 concludes the letter by encouraging the Colossians to be in prayer with one another, for Paul, and also for others who are spreading Christ's message. He also urges them to consider how they speak and act toward those who are outside of their Christian community.

Notes:

Notes:

Theological Underpinnings

It's important to study and understand our roots, remaining connected with our community, and making sure to always remember Christ as the head of our lives. When we look to Christ's life, we understand better how we are to live; we understand the mystery of how his death and resurrection reconcile us to God; we see how with Christ it is possible for us to overcome the habits and inclinations that separate us from God; and we instead live as people who love and serve one another out of our love for God.

Applying the Lesson to Your Own Life

Have you ever needed to be reminded of who you are? Is there a time when you wondered if your faith was stronger earlier in your journey than it is today? Have you ever been overwhelmed by the many messages the world pours into you and needed someone to remind you of why you believe what you believe, and what it means for your life? Have you ever needed redirection? Paul writes this letter to the Colossians as a wake-up call, a plea for them to return to their identity and their mission amidst the false teachings and philosophies filling their society.

The Lesson

 ## Get Started (15 min.)

Call to Worship

As students enter, have the song, "Beloved" by Derek Webb playing. Invite students to go around the room and answer the questions on the newsprint:

1. What is your role in your family?
2. What is your role in the church?
3. What is your role at school/in your friendships?

Call to Wake Up: "Guess Who? Live"

Ask everyone in the room to stand.

Select a volunteer to begin as the leader. The leader will choose one person in the room to be "the person" and does not tell anyone (including the person) who it is. One at a time, students raise their hands to ask a "yes" or "no" question to the leader about the selected person.

For example, "Is the person wearing glasses?"

If the answer is no, all the people wearing glasses may sit down. If the answer is yes, everyone who is NOT wearing glasses may sit down. Even if a person sits down, they can still participate in the game.

The questions and answers continue until the person's identity is discovered (or they are the only person left standing). If you want, you can add a limit to the number of questions the group is allowed to ask to make it more challenging.

If time permits, repeat the game.

 **Listen Up (20 min.)**

Divide the students into four groups. Assign one chapter from Colossians to each group. Ask each group to consider these questions as they read their chapter:
- What is Paul telling the Colossians in this chapter?
- What does this chapter tell you about Jesus?
- What does this chapter tell you about followers of Jesus?

Option 1

Once students have read the chapter and considered the questions together, have the whole group come back together and share what they learned in each chapter.

Notes:

Notes:

Option 2

Once students have read the chapter and considered the questions together in their groups, have each group draw a picture to represent what they learned in their chapter, and then come together to share it with everyone.

# Now What? (10 min.)

Option 1

Watch the video, "Knowing My Identity" from BluefishTV. Invite students to share their thoughts on the video.

Discussion Question:
- Who or what competes with Jesus for your identity?

Allow students time to share stories and examples from their lives.

Option 2

Listen again to the song, "Beloved" by Derek Webb. Display the lyrics to the song. Allow them time to listen to the song.

Invite students to share their thoughts on the song.

Discussion Question:
- Who or what are the "salesmen and thieves" competing for your attention and identity?

Allow students time to share stories and examples from their lives.

Option 3

Together, write a letter to your church. Use Paul's format in his letter to the Colossian church. Consider together the frustrations the youth have within the church family or other struggles the church is facing. Respond to these together in a letter. When finished decide how (or if) you will share the letter with the church.

Example:
Dear _____ Church,
We thank God for you because…
We pray that you remember…
We know you struggle with…

Christ has overcome that by…
Here's how we're going to be with you in our struggle together…
Focus on these things…
We love you.

 ## Live It (15 min.)

Give each student a strip of cloth. Invite them to write on the cloth something that tends to steal their attention or threatens their identity as a follower of Christ. When they're finished, tell them to place their strip on the table (or choose another hard, smooth surface within your space). When everyone has had an opportunity to bring their cloth forward, direct the hair dryer at the gathered strips of cloth and turn it on full blast, blowing the strips off the table.

Instruct the students to retrieve their strips.

Read Colossians 3:12-17, and bring out the brick on which you have written the qualities outlined in this passage.

Invite students to write on the other side of their strip of cloth one of these qualities that would help them in their struggle to maintain their identity in Christ, or one they would like to focus on improving.

When everyone is finished, instruct students to bring their

Notes:

Notes:

strips, and gather in a circle for prayer. Put the brick in the middle of the circle, and have the hairdryer close by. Beginning with your own strip, silently take the strip of the person next to you and tie it to yours, then pass the tied strips to that person and allow them to do the same, tying on the following person's strip, and continue around the circle until a garland of all the strips returns to you. Once everyone's strips are tied together, tie the garland to the brick. Then turn the hairdryer on full blast, demonstrating that the strips can no longer fly away.

Close with this benediction:
May we go from this place strengthened by one another, ready to serve one another, and rooted in our love of Jesus Christ, who continually restores our relationship with God. Amen.

© 2014 Discipleship Ministry Team of the Ministry Council of the Cumberland Presbyterian Church. All Rights Reserved.